DEADLY DANGEROUS
KINGS AND QUEENS

KARL SHAW

A&C Black • London

Published 2012 by A&C Black
An imprint of Bloomsbury Publishing Plc
50 Bedford Square, London, WC1B 3DP

www.acblack.com
www.bloomsbury.com

ISBN 978-1-4081-6568-3

Designed by Marcus Duck

A CIP record for this book is available from the British Library.

This book is produced using paper made from wood grown in managed, sustainable forests. It is natural, renewable and recyclable. The logging and manufacturing processes conform to the environmental regulations of the country of origin.

Printed and bound by CPI Group (UK) Ltd, Croydon, CR0 4YY.

1 3 5 7 9 10 8 6 4 2

CONTENTS

THE KINGS WHOSE NAMES NOBODY COULD SPELL

Before 1066 the English crown, the oldest in the world, was worn by various Egberts, Eadwigs, Aethlreds, Aethlwulfs, Aethelbalds and Ethelstans, none of whom was very memorable because nobody could agree how to spell their names.

To be fair this wouldn't have bothered many of their subjects, because very few of them could read or write anyway. Besides, they had more important things to worry about, like coping with disease, or famine, or how to avoid getting hacked to death by those vicious Viking invaders who were running around the country, murdering and looting at will.

There was just one king whom everyone remembered. Out of this spelling nightmare emerged Alfred 'the Great' (although in fact he was only the king of half of England – the southern bit, as far north as the Midlands). Alfred was a strong king who stopped the Viking raids by building a navy and a well-trained army. He also tried to rule fairly and encouraged people to learn. There wasn't very much Alfred couldn't do. He was pretty rubbish at baking, but TV cookery shows were another 1100 years away so people didn't really care if he burnt cakes or not.

For a while England was peaceful and happy, but when Alfred died things went downhill again. The country was ruled by more weak kings – most of them with difficult names. England was in an almost constant state of civil war due to pushy local barons who thought they could do a better job than the king.

Meanwhile, to make matters even worse, the Vikings started raiding again, because England was now a dangerously divided kingdom and a great target for attack. In 1042, England found itself under yet another useless king, Edward 'the Confessor', who spent most of his time praying instead of improving England's defences.

By now most people were thinking the same thing.

'If only we had another strong king like Alfred, someone who doesn't take any nonsense from anyone. Then we could all have a bit of peace and quiet.'

Be careful what you wish for!

THE KING WHO MADE A LIST

William I was descended from a much-feared Viking warrior called Rollo, a man who was said to be so big that there wasn't a horse strong enough to take his weight. William had a lot of Rollo's Viking character. His idea of fun was skinning his enemies alive then chopping their hands off.[1] William was just the sort of person to knock some sense into those silly, feuding English just across the channel.

William already had a dodgy claim to the English throne as a distant relative of Edward 'the Confessor'. He had a stroke of luck in 1064 when the future King of England, Harold, was sailing down the English Channel and his ship blew off course and landed in Normandy. William took Harold prisoner and tricked him into swearing an oath of loyalty to William over a pile of saints' bones, hidden under a table. Harold did as he was told, but then forgot all about it when he got back home. When

1 He did this once to some people who insulted him by calling him the son of a tanner's daughter – which was another thing he was very touchy about. A tanner worked with leather by soaking it in dog poo.

Edward 'the Confessor' died in 1066, Harold had himself crowned King of England. William was furious; now there was some conquering to be done.

William and his army landed on the beach at Hastings on 28th September. William's bad temper was made even worse when he tripped as he stepped off his boat, fell headfirst onto the beach and swallowed a mouthful of sand. Nobody laughed.

However, the showdown with Harold would have to wait, as Harold's army were in the north of England fighting off yet another Viking invasion. Harold won, but some of his best men were killed and the rest of the army had to trek all the way back down south. By the time they got to Hastings they were already exhausted. William meanwhile was having a good time chilling on the beach, throwing the odd peasant on the barbecue.

Careful, you'll have someone's eye out with that.

Harold's army came very close to

winning, but in the end tiredness took its toll and they were defeated. Harold was killed by an arrow through his eye, but the Norman soldiers also cut his head off and chopped his arms off – just to make sure. By the time they had finished, Harold was so badly mutilated that his wife Edith couldn't identify him.

William was crowned king on Christmas Day in Westminster Abbey. A cheer went up as the crown was placed on his head. The Norman guards outside thought something had gone horribly wrong, so they started attacking the crowd and set fire to several buildings.

William's first job as the new king was to take his army on a tour of England to let everyone know who was in charge. They destroyed everything in their path. If anyone complained, the punishments were terrible. However, another thing William did was get rid of capital punishment.

'Hurrah, no more hangings!'

'That's right. I'm going to chop off your hands and blind you instead. I want you alive so everyone can see who they're messing with'

When William stopped blinding people and chopping their limbs off long enough to draw breath, he thought that it might be handy to have a list of everything he had just conquered. In 1086 he sent out a team of surveyors to compile a great book of every single bit of property in his new kingdom – the Domesday Book.

Sadly, William didn't live long enough to enjoy reading it (not that he could read anyway). At the ripe old age of 60, after surviving a lifetime of almost endless warring and bloodletting, he was riding through the streets of a town he had just burned to the ground when his horse stumbled on some hot cinders, giving William fatal injuries.

His funeral was even crazier than his coronation. William had grown very fat and the stone coffin prepared for him was too small. After a lot of poking and prodding as they tried to cram him in, his bowels burst open, filling the church with an 'intolerable stench' and the mourners fled for the doors.

This time people did laugh.

THE KING WHO DIED IN A HUNTING ACCIDENT

When William I died he had kingdoms on both sides of the Channel. He surprised everyone by giving his old homeland Normandy to his eldest son Robert and England to Robert's younger brother William. For Robert this was like waking up on Christmas morning and finding that your parents had given you a nice new mobile phone, only to discover that your little brother has been given the very latest games console. You just knew it would end in tears.

William II was quite short[2] with red hair and a foul temper which made him red-faced with anger – either of

2 Rufus's mother Queen Matilda was only 4' 2" tall. As William I was over 6' tall they must have made a very odd looking couple.

which could have accounted for his nickname 'Rufus' (the red). In one respect Rufus was just like his father – if you crossed him he wouldn't think twice about ripping your ears off and nailing them to the front door. Unusually for the time, Rufus wasn't very religious and didn't spend large sums of money on building new churches, unlike his father. In fact, when Rufus was short of cash he simply raided the nearest monastery.

The most memorable event in his life was his death, which was one of the great 'whodunits' in history.

In the 11th century, the royal family liked to relax by killing wild animals. One day Rufus was out hunting in the forest with a few friends, including his younger brother Henry (who didn't get the mobile phone or the games console). Rufus 'accidentally' stepped in front of an arrow fired by a Frenchman called Walter Tirel and it hit the king in the chest. Seeing that Rufus was lifeless and bleeding, Tirel panicked, jumped on his horse and fled for his life. It was left to a few passing peasants to bundle the dead king on a cart and take him to Winchester, dripping blood all the way.

Was Rufus's death an accident? At first, everyone thought so. Fatal hunting accidents happened all the time. However, the finger of suspicion was soon pointed at

Henry. Rufus didn't have any children, so when he died his older brother Robert of Normandy was the favourite to become king. Perhaps Henry had Rufus killed so he could grab the throne before Robert turned up? Henry vanished just before the 'accident' happened and was already on his way to Westminster to have himself crowned king, seizing his dead brother's treasury on the way. Brotherly love doesn't seem to have featured very much in the Norman royal family.

THE KING WHO WAS KILLED BY A FISH SUPPER

After the two much-hated Williams, the new King Henry I thought it would be a good idea if he tried to make himself more popular.

Unlike Rufus, Henry was born in England, which went down well with all of his Anglo-Saxon subjects. He also promised to overturn some of the extreme punishments handed out by his brother – like digging your eyes out if you stole a rabbit.

However, he couldn't help feeling that his oldest brother, Duke Robert of Normandy, still hadn't got over that whole mobile phone/games console thing. Henry's suspicions were confirmed when Robert landed an invasion army in Portsmouth. Robert was hoping for support from the English barons, but the support never showed up. Henry had already bought their loyalty by promising not to make them pay heavy taxes. In the end, Henry and Robert met in peace and Robert gave up his claim to the English throne in exchange for some of the land Henry owned in Normandy.

But Henry still didn't really trust his big brother to keep his side of the bargain, so a few years later he invaded Normandy and had Robert thrown into prison. To make sure he stayed put, he had Robert's eyes burned out.

Henry's only son, William, had drowned in the English Channel on his way back from fighting in Normandy. It still left him with a daughter, Matilda, married to a Frenchman, and a couple of grandchildren.

In 1135 Henry went to France to visit his grandchildren and got into an argument with his daughter and son-in-law about who would be the next king. The story goes that after a day's hunting Henry sat down in his son-in-law's house to his favourite meal, a plate of grilled lampreys.

'Anyone fancy sharing my lampreys?'

'What's a lamprey?'

'A blood-sucking fish with rows of pointy teeth.'

'Er, no thanks, I think I'll stick to cod and chips'.

Just as he finished his meal, Henry keeled over and died. One explanation was that he had eaten so many lampreys he literally died of overeating. Another version says that the lampreys had gone 'off' and he died of food poisoning.

Considering Henry's difficult relationship with his family, you can't help thinking that there was something fishy about the whole business.

FOUL FACT

Henry I was the first of three British kings who were supposed to have been killed by overeating. King John was said to have died after eating too many peaches. King George I died after stuffing his face with melons.

THE KING WHO KILLED AN ARCHBISHOP

When Henry I died he left his daughter, Matilda as his successor. In the Middle Ages, equal opportunities for women hadn't yet caught on and England's powerful barons really didn't like being ruled by a woman. They supported Henry's cousin Stephen. England was thrown into a brutal civil war known as 'the anarchy'. Everyone was relieved when Stephen died and the crown passed to Matilda's grandson Henry. England now had its first Plantagenet king.

'Great, but what exactly is a Plantagenet?'

'Well the new king's father had a habit of wearing a sprig of broom in his hat – in Latin *planta genista* or Plantagenet.'

'Oh right. That's a bit weird isn't it?'

'Just be thankful he isn't another Norman!'

Henry II was a fair and wise king and introduced important new laws. Up until now, the usual way of deciding whether a person was innocent or guilty had been a method called 'trial by ordeal'. The accused had to walk barefoot across red-hot metal or pluck a stone out of a boiling cauldron. If their blisters had cleared up within three days, it was a sign from God that they were innocent. It goes without saying that there weren't many 'not guilty' verdicts. Henry replaced this painful system with a jury of 12 men, who would decide if the person was guilty or innocent without the need for blisters.

Despite all of this good work Henry had a terrible temper, which would get him into serious trouble. He got into frequent arguments with the Church, who didn't like being told what to do by the king. In 1162, Henry persuaded an old friend called Thomas Becket to become the new Archbishop of Canterbury. Henry thought that his friend would support him in Church matters, but to his surprise, Becket did just the opposite. Henry flew into one of his famous rages and said, 'Will no-one rid me of this priest?'

Four knights, eager to please the king, rode off to Canterbury and bashed Becket's head in, spilling his brains all over the floor of the Cathedral in full view of a crowd of worshippers. This did serious damage to Henry's good name.

Henry claimed it was all a big mistake and he never meant Becket to be harmed. He pleaded to the Pope for forgiveness. As a punishment, the Pope ordered Henry to crawl to Canterbury Cathedral on his hands and knees, there to be whipped by monks. Becket's murder did Canterbury Cathedral no harm at all and it became a more popular tourist attraction than Alton Towers.[3]

Henry had founded a new royal dynasty that would last for another 330 years, but it wasn't going to be plain sailing for the Plantagenets. He had eight children, including five sons who constantly squabbled about who was going to inherit what.

Henry died in 1189 of grief, it was said, after watching his family slowly fall apart. This was a bit of poetic licence on the part of historians. What the king really died of was dysentery – an infection of the bowels, resulting in death by severe diarrhoea. Not very poetic, that.

---

3 Which to be fair wasn't all that difficult, because at the time Alton Towers was just a field full of sheep somewhere near Stoke.

FOUL FACT

Henry II kept a court jester called Roland who was required to fart for the amusement of his guests at the annual Christmas Day banquet.

THE KING WHO WAS NEVER THERE

King Richard 'the Lionheart' is remembered as a great English hero, which is amazing for someone who spoke only French and spent only seven months of his entire 10-year reign in England.

Richard had Anglo-French parents and thought more of himself as a Frenchman with a second home in England – one he didn't visit very often and only then so he could get money from his subjects to go off and fight another foreign war.

Richard was very good at fighting foreign wars but he wasn't very good at anything else. The big story of his kingship was a war called the Third Crusade. Richard took a huge army to the Holy Lands to free the city of Jerusalem which had been taken by the Muslim warrior Saladin. The war cost a huge amount of money and almost bankrupted the country. In the end, the king was reduced to selling off bits of northern England to the

Scots. He joked that he would even sell London if only he could find a buyer.

In 1199, Richard was attacking a castle in France, so confident of victory that he was casually wandering along the castle walls without his armour on, when he was hit in the shoulder by a crossbow bolt fired by one of the castle's defenders. It didn't kill him, but the wound became badly infected when his surgeon tried to pull the bolt out and Richard died from the effects of gangrene.

The person who shot him was a French youth called Pierre Basile. When Basile was caught, he told his captors that he had tried to kill the king in revenge because the English had killed his brother and his father. Richard was so touched by this story that he forgave Basile and ordered him to be set free with a cash gift of 100 shillings. That's the legend.

Unfortunately, what really happened was a less happy ending for the French youth. As soon as Richard was dead, his men stormed the castle and executed the French defenders by hanging them from the ramparts – all except young Pierre Basile, who was skinned alive then hanged, his punishment for shooting the king.

THE KING WHO LOST THE CROWN JEWELS IN THE WASH

The reign of King Richard I, who was never there, was followed by that of his brother John, who was there a bit too much for anyone's liking.

John was a bad king. There was a clue to this in his nickname – King John 'the Bad'. People already had a fairly good idea of what to expect from his reign because while his brother was off fighting abroad, John was taking care of business at home. He quickly made his mark as a useless and greedy ruler. He is most famous as the villain in the legend of Robin Hood.

Robin was the first ever superhero. He wore a costume, fought injustice and had a secret identity. Some people say he was a Saxon lord fighting the Normans, others say that he was an ordinary man who became an outlaw after shooting one of the king's deer. Either way, he was popular because he supported King Richard against his terrible brother John.

Like Robin Hood, John was very interested in the redistribution of wealth, but unlike Robin he stole from rich and poor alike and gave to himself. He was also very disloyal to his absent brother. When Richard was captured on his way home from the Third Crusade by one of his enemies, John refused to pay the £60,000 ransom to free him (and even offered a bribe to keep Richard in prison). Just to rub everyone's noses in it, the ransom was eventually raised by a massive tax increase for everyone in the country.

Richard was freed, only to die a short time later fighting in France. Now John was king in his own right, he also proved himself to be a useless military leader and he lost nearly all of his lands in France. This terrible defeat, which cut the Norman barons of England off from their old homeland, was more than they could take. In 1215 the barons cornered John and made him sign the Magna Carta, or Great Charter. It was a document forcing the king to obey the law and to be fair to his subjects.

The Magna Carta is now seen as a very important piece of English history, but at the time it was just a power-grab by the barons. John had no intention of sticking to his promises. He only signed it to get himself out of a tricky situation. The barons didn't trust him to keep his word either. They were quietly making plans to invite the French king's son Louis to invade England and take over the throne. However, in October 1216, John settled the matter by dying.

According to legend, John was crossing the marshy area known as The Wash and lost his baggage, including the Crown Jewels, to the incoming tide. This loss apparently affected John's health and a few days later he died from dysentery at Newark. Soon after his death, rumours started that poisoned cider, poisoned plums or 'a surfeit of peaches' had finished him off. Poison or dysentery? We'll never know.

With John dead, the barons decided to support his nine-year-old son, who was crowned King Henry III[4]. So we didn't end up with a King Louis I after all, which is why so many of us are now still rubbish at speaking French.

4 They had to use his mother's tiara instead – the actual crown was lost in The Wash.

THE KING WHO HAMMERED THE SCOTS (AND THE WELSH)

From 1232 England had three King Edwards in a row.[5] The first Edward was a huge, towering figure known as 'Longshanks'. Several kings were known for their bad tempers – but Edward's temper was the worst of all. His terrible tantrums and his massive build made him a truly terrifying figure. The story goes that the Dean of St Paul's, who wanted to complain to Edward about high taxes, was so frightened when he came face to face with the king that he had a heart attack and fell down dead. Another time Edward erupted in anger during a family row and tore handfuls of his son's hair out.

Most of the time, Edward saved his anger for the battlefield. Wales had only been half-conquered by the

5 There had already been Anglo-Saxon King Edwards, but all kings are numbered from one upwards after 1066.

Normans. When Llewellyn ap Gruffydd led an uprising, Edward finally settled the matter by invading Wales with a huge army and then covering it with castles.

After his soldiers had finished torturing and slaughtering the Welsh and burning their homes, he showed them that he also had a gentle, caring side by giving his eldest son the title Prince of Wales.

As it turned out, the Welsh got off quite lightly compared to the Scots. In 1296 Edward took advantage of a vacant throne north of the border and simply declared himself King of Scotland. When the Scots complained, Edward invaded and handed out the same vicious punishment he'd just given the Welsh.

It didn't all go Edward's way at first. On 11th September 1297, the Scots defeated the English at the Battle of Stirling Bridge. The Scots were overjoyed. However, eventually Edward won the war and the defeated Scots rebel leader William Wallace got the full treatment. He was dragged through the streets of London behind a horse, then hanged, but taken down from the scaffold while he was still alive. Then his entrails were cut out and burned and his arms, legs and head were chopped off. His arms and legs were sent to Scotland, while his head was mounted on London Bridge.

Edward was setting off north to put down yet another Scottish rebellion in 1307 when he died aged 68. He was buried in a plain black marble tomb, painted with the Latin words *Scottorum malleus* – Hammer of the Scots.

THE KING WHO WON THE 'MOST GRUESOME DEATH' AWARD

Several kings and queens suffered some really strange and nasty deaths.

For example:

- the Saxon king Edmund, tied to a tree and used as target practice by Danish archers
- Edmund II, stabbed to death while he sat on the toilet
- King Harold, chopped to pieces by Normans at the Battle of Hastings
- Richard I, died of gangrene when he was shot by an arrow and the wound turned septic
- Richard II, smothered or strangled in his sleep
- James I of Scotland, stabbed 28 times while trying to escape down a drain

Poor Edward II is remembered for enduring the most gruesome death of them all. From the beginning of his reign, he wasn't a popular king. England was going through a bad time because of a series of terrible harvests. He also lived in the considerable shadow of his father, who had spent most of his time winning great victories on the battlefield against the Scots. Young Edward didn't care much about fighting anyone. He was too busy having a good time hanging out with his friends at court, especially his favourite, a young French courtier called Piers Gaveston.

The barons thought the king should be listening to them, not his friends. They really hated Gaveston, especially when the king started to shower him with gifts and titles. In 1312, a group of barons lynched then executed him, leaving his headless body by the roadside.

With his friend dead, Edward's attention moved on to another young court favourite, Hugh Despenser.

'Er, I'm a bit worried about this job title – 'king's favourite'.'

'What's the problem?'

'Didn't the last one have his head cut off?'

Sure enough, Edward's new friendship also got up the noses of his English barons. It didn't go down too well either with his neglected wife Queen Isabelle. Edward was 23 when he got married to her, and she was just 12. Compared to some royal marriages, this wasn't thought to be too much of an age gap. Edward had already been engaged to a three-year-old princess, but she died when she was seven! But the queen was no longer a young girl, but a woman with a wicked temper, known as 'Isabelle the she-wolf'. With one of her husband's sworn enemies, a baron called Roger Mortimer, she plotted to get rid of Edward.

Mortimer and Isabella raised money for an army and invaded England to widespread cheering – the first

successful invasion since 1066. Edward and Despenser fled to Wales, where they were captured three weeks later. Despenser was stripped naked in front of a screaming mob, strung up, then his innards were cut out and his head was cut off. Isabelle and Mortimer had a picnic as they watched.

Edward was taken as a prisoner to Berkeley Castle in Gloucestershire. There he was tortured, then suffocated, then to finish him off they shoved a red-hot poker up his bum.

Edward's screams could be heard for miles around.

THE KING WHO BANNED FOOTBALL

The third Edward became king aged just 15, but he didn't let his youth and inexperience hold him back. In 1333, he won another great victory over the Scots – and he was still only a teenager.

This was very impressive stuff. However, beating the Welsh and the Scots was one thing (okay, two if you want to be picky), but if you really wanted to be remembered as a great English king you had to inflict a crushing defeat on the French. And that's exactly what Edward III did – with knobs on.

Edward was desperate for a fight with the French. In 1337, he tried to start a war by declaring himself King of France, but the French just ignored him. But in 1340, Edward found an excuse to invade France – to protect England's wool trade in Flanders.[6]

---

6 In the Middle Ages, wool was big business and the king could raise a lot of money by slapping heavy taxes on the export of it.

One thing that the English had brought home from the wars in Wales (apart from a few sticks of rock with Llandudno written through them) was their deadly longbows. They could fire iron-tipped armour-piercing arrows 250 yards with murderous accuracy. It took years to learn to fire a longbow properly, so the king banned football so everyone could spend more time on archery practice.

Edward finally got to try his longbows out for real on several thousand French knights at the battle of Crecy in 1346. The French didn't know what hit them: they rode into a hailstorm of arrows, according to a French chronicler, 'so dense that it blotted out the sun'. Although the French army was much bigger, by the end of the day Edward had won a famous victory.

Edward's 50-year reign was mostly a good time for England. It defeated its old enemies, the Scots and the French. English replaced Latin and French as the official national language. The Houses of Parliament, the Lords and the Commons, were created. England even had a new patron saint – St. George. However, there was one thing that ruined Edward's otherwise successful reign; it was called the Black Death.

'This *Black* Death. It isn't a very pleasant name, couldn't we call it something else. We don't want to start a panic, do we?'

'We could call it death by swellings under the armpits and in the groin, oozing blood and pus, until the body becomes covered in dark blotches, accompanied by intense headaches, nausea and vomiting.'

'Right, the Black Death it is then!'

The disease arrived in Dorset in 1348 and it soon reached London. No part of the British Isles escaped. Eventually, it wiped out almost half of Edward's subjects.

The reign ended badly for Edward personally as well. He had a beautiful and popular wife, but she died young, so he took a mistress whom nobody liked and it made him unpopular. His eldest son, the Black Prince, died in 1376, and Edward followed him the year after.

FOUL FACT

When the Black Death was at its peak, the Scots decided that it would be a great time to invade England. They believed that the disease was God's punishment for the English and that the Scots couldn't catch it. They only realised the flaw in their plan when their army started to drop dead in their thousands. So they retreated, taking it back home with them to Scotland where it killed even more people.

THE KING WHO WAS A WASTE OF SPACE

When Edward III died, the crown passed to his 10-year-old grandson, Richard II. At first everyone said how cute the new young king was. They were very patient with him, stuck his drawings on the kitchen wall and smiled if he threw a temper tantrum because he couldn't stay up late or invade France.

Early in his reign, he passed a big challenge with flying colours. It was a difficult time because the Black Death was followed by terrible hardship. It all kicked off when Richard's government imposed a very unpopular Poll Tax. In 1381, a mob of thousands of angry peasants led by Wat Tyler ran riot, smashing windows and looting shops. The king's advisers were terrified when the mob marched towards London.

'Sire, the peasants are revolting'

'Tell me about it. I've heard they don't even use a handkerchief!'[7]

The 14-year-old Richard rode out to meet the mob and listen to their complaints. Everyone agreed that the young king had been really brave in standing up to them on his own (all right, well, he did have a few armed knights as back-up) and that he played a big part in stopping the rebellion.[8]

Unfortunately, Richard's handling of the Peasants' Revolt was the high point of his reign. When he got a bit older, everyone's patience with him started to wear thin. He started behaving like a stroppy teenager and went into a big sulk if everyone didn't call him Your Majesty (he was the first king to insist on this). He was also keen to remind people that God had appointed him as king. He seemed to have forgotten that he only got the job because his ancestor William I had seized the crown by chopping the previous owner into pieces.

---

7 Richard didn't just use a handkerchief – he invented it!

8 It didn't go quite so well for Wat Tyler, who was killed and his head placed on a spike.

Richard was more interested in dressing up than running the country, and very strangely for the 14th century, he had baths. He used a spoon to eat soup! And he didn't seem at all keen on the idea of killing people in foreign countries. People began to wonder if he was mad. On the streets of London, he was pelted with rubbish when his parade rode by.

In the end it was a challenge from his own family, not a popular revolt, which removed him from the throne. The king's undoing was an argument with his cousin, Henry of Lancaster, whom Richard had kicked out of the country. In 1399, Henry returned to England with an army of supporters. Richard was defeated on the battlefield and taken prisoner by the rebel army. His cousin was crowned Henry IV, the first king of the new royal house of Lancaster.

By the time of Henry's coronation, Richard was already dead, murdered at the age of 32 at Pontefract Castle in Yorkshire. Some say that he was smothered or strangled in his sleep. Others say that he was starved to death. Either way, Richard was dead by early February 1400 when his body was taken to London and put on display at St. Paul's Cathedral.

FOUL FACT

Richard spent ages designing a great tomb for himself in Westminster Abbey. In the early 1800s, a schoolboy poked his hand through a hole in the side of Richard's coffin and took his jawbone home as a souvenir. His dad put it in a glass case and labelled it proudly 'Jawbone of Richard II.'

THE KING WHO MARRIED A WITCH

There were a couple of bad omens at Henry IV's coronation. The first was when one of his golden spurs fell off. This was said to be a sure sign that there would be a rebellion. The second was when the crown was placed on his head and they found that his hair was crawling with head lice. This was said to be a sure sign that he had nits.

Having gained the crown by violence, Henry IV spent his entire reign looking over his shoulder, wondering when someone was going to try to overthrow him. He was so nervous about all the plots to kill him that he slept in his suit of armour. Henry also suffered from a terrible skin disorder, which people thought was God's punishment for stealing the crown from his cousin.

Henry also had a very unpopular wife, a French widow called Joan of Navarre. Joan was obviously bad news, because she was the daughter of Charles 'the Bad'. On the other hand, she was also the granddaughter of John 'the

Good', but bad news is always more likely to make the headlines. Joan was so unpopular that she was accused of being a witch.

As if having terrible acne and being married to a witch wasn't bad enough, Henry also suffered terrible headaches and had fits, possibly due to the many blows to the head received in his years of jousting. He had a very bad fit whilst praying at the shrine of Edward the Confessor in Westminster Abbey at Christmas. It was so bad that everyone thought he was dead. When the king recovered from his fit, he realised that his crown was missing. When he looked around to see where it had gone, he found his eldest son trying it on for size!

His son had to wait a further three years before he got to wear it for keeps, when Henry had another, this time fatal, fit.

THE KING WITH THE VERY BAD HAIRCUT

Henry V came to the throne when he was just 17 years old. On the day of his coronation, there was a terrible snowstorm. This time people couldn't make their minds up whether it was a good omen or a bad omen.

'Er, perhaps it's a sign of bad weather?'

Henry was tall and powerfully built. In his portrait we see only the left side of his face, to hide an ugly scar left by an arrow wound. He was a very religious king and he spent a lot of time praying. He had his hair cut in a pudding-bowl style, which made him look like a priest or a monk.

There was a very cruel side to Henry. He hanged his own soldiers for incredibly small offences. Once, at a meeting of the English and French, the soldiers were told to stay behind their fences. For a dare, a young English soldier jumped over the fence and jumped back again. He was hanged on the spot for ignoring the king's order.

By this time, Parliament had forgotten how expensive wars were, so England had another go at invading France. Besides, this might be the perfect time to pick a fight with her neighbour across the Channel.

'Hmm, what do you make of this new king of France, Charles 'the Mad?'

'I'm not sure, sire. You don't suppose there might be a clue somewhere in his name?'[9]

Although his reign was quite short, Henry is remembered as one of the great English kings because of his victory over the French, against the odds. By the time his army finally came face to face with the French at Agincourt in 1415, he had already lost a third of his army to disease and was outnumbered by at least four to one.

Luckily, the French army got stuck in the Agincourt mud. Henry's longbow men picked them off at will,

9 King Charles VI of France did indeed live up to his nickname. He went around his palace howling like a wolf and was convinced that his legs were made of glass and they might shatter. They put him in a padded cell after he killed four of his courtiers for fun.

while his knights hacked them to death where they stood in their heavy armour, waist deep in mud. It was like the Glastonbury festival, only worse.

Henry V died of dysentery, just outside Paris, having never seen his only son, who was born while he was away fighting. The king's body was boiled in a cauldron and chopped up before it was shipped home. His cask was also filled with sweet-smelling incense – which was just as well, because it was two months before he could be buried.

THE KING WHO HAD HIS NEPHEWS MURDERED

The reign of Richard III was one of the shortest and most infamous of all the British kings and queens. It began with the sudden death of his older brother King Edward IV in 1483.

When he was a young man Edward was tall, handsome and very fit, but he was also very fond of eating. By the time he was 40, he was extremely fat. In 1483, he had a heart attack on a fishing trip and died (although one historian recorded that the king died from eating too much fruit and veg!).

Edward's death came at a really bad time for the country because the king had only recently declared war on France (again).

His son, the new King Edward V, was only 12 years old. So the new boy-king's kindly uncle Richard had a great idea.

Why don't you let me take care of the lad – just for a short while until he's old enough to rule? Parliament agreed. Just two weeks later, Richard had Edward and his 10-year-old brother Richard placed in the Tower of London 'for their protection'. Even now, nobody suspected that Richard was up to no good. Perhaps they should.

'This Richard... isn't he the one who had his own brother the Duke of Clarence drowned in a barrel of wine?'

With the first and second in line to the throne safely under lock and key, Richard persuaded Parliament to give him the crown instead of his nephew. Parliament wasn't happy about this, but Richard was in too strong a position for anyone to argue, especially given his recent habit of beheading anyone who crossed him.

The princes were never seen again. As time went by it became obvious that something terrible had happened to them. In fact they were already dead – probably killed by being smothered in their sleep with pillows - and almost certainly on Richard's orders.

William Shakespeare wrote a play about Richard III showing him as a sort of evil, twisted hunchback. Other writers went even further by claiming that when Richard was born he was covered with black hair, like some sort of monster. Neither image was right. He didn't have a hunchback, or a limp, or a problem with unsightly body hair, although he might have had one shoulder a bit higher than the other. So he wasn't actually an evil monster. But he was almost certainly a murderer and if he thought that would make him a popular king he was very much mistaken.

Rumours about the deaths of the princes in the tower spread. Richard became the most hated man in the country and rebellions against him sprang up everywhere. The king's opponents rallied behind the late king's distant Welsh relative Henry Tudor.

Opposing armies led by Richard III and Henry Tudor met at the battle of Bosworth Field, near Leicester. Although outnumbered, Henry's forces won and Richard III became the very last British king to die in battle. According to legend, the crown was found under a hawthorn bush and was then placed on the head of Henry, who then became King Henry VII.

Nobody was really sure what had become of the two princes until 150 years later, when workmen demolishing a staircase in the Tower of London found a wooden chest. Inside were the bones of the two small boys.

THE KING WHO EMPLOYED A BOTTOM WIPER

The Tudor dynasty opened for business with Henry VII, who was just killing time until the arrival of his much more famous son. In fact the seventh Henry was quite a successful king, but this tends to get overlooked when your son is an overweight, unstable wife-killer with a nasty habit of beheading anyone who didn't let him have his own way.[10]

The best known portraits of Henry VIII show a fat, bloated, bearded man in tights, so it is quite difficult to imagine him as he was when he first came to the throne, a very handsome, sporty young man who played tennis, wrote poetry and composed songs.

10 His father Henry VII was quite memorable for one thing. He liked to show off his favourite souvenir to his guests – St. George's left leg. This must have been quite a conversation opener.

There were two big themes in Henry's reign. The first was the way he dealt with anyone who crossed him. During his 38-year reign, he had about 72,000 people put to death. This was mostly by burning or beheading. Henry did invent a new method of execution for Richard Rosse, cook to the Bishop of Rochester, who had poisoned the soup at a banquet and killed 17 people. The king had him boiled to death in one of his own cooking pots.

The second was his obsession with having a healthy son to secure the future of his new Tudor dynasty – a problem known as The King's Great Matter.

♛

Henry married six times. His first wife was a Spanish lady, Catherine of Aragon. They were happily married for nearly 20 years and she gave him a daughter, but not the son Henry wanted. Because the Pope wouldn't let Henry divorce her, he split from the Pope and founded a new Church of England. When Catherine died, Henry celebrated with a banquet.

Despite the enormous amount of trouble Henry had gone through to marry his second wife Anne Boleyn, she didn't give him a son either. He also suspected she was being unfaithful to him, so he had her beheaded for treason. He had every angle covered: if that charge didn't stick, he was going to have her burned as a witch because she had 12 fingers. While Anne Boleyn was being beheaded, Henry VIII went off for a game of tennis.

His third wife Jane Seymour did give him a son, but she died soon after.

And so he moved swiftly on to wife number four, a German princess called Anne of Cleves. He had been pleased with her portrait, but when she arrived for the wedding, it turned out she wasn't quite as beautiful in the flesh. In fact, she looked like a horse. They were quickly divorced, but at least Anne got to keep her head.

Catherine Howard was his fifth wife. He was more than 30 years older than her and by this time weighed 28st. He had her head removed in 1542, aged only 17, because she had an affair with one of Henry's courtiers, Thomas Culpeper. When accused, Catherine said defiantly, 'I die a queen, but I would rather have died the wife of Culpeper.'

Within the year Henry married the last and luckiest of all his wives, Catherine Parr. She had been married twice before, but kept her head and married again after Henry's death.

When the Pope fell out with Henry, he was so annoyed that he excommunicated the king – in other words, Henry was damned to Hell for all eternity. But hey, every cloud has a silver lining! Henry quickly spotted that as head of the new Church of England he could do pretty much as he liked with all of the Church's lands and properties – so he nabbed the lot for himself and sold them for cash.

By the end of his life Henry was grossly fat and in terrible pain from his swollen legs. He had to be carried around in a chair and hoisted up and down stairs by pulleys. He died aged 56, a fat and diseased – but very wealthy – king.

FOUL FACT

Henry VIII employed a servant with the title Groom Of The Stool. It was his job to wipe the royal backside.

THE QUEEN WHO BURNED PEOPLE ALIVE

Henry VIII was succeeded by his nine-year-old son, who ruled as Edward VI. Edward was a very frail and sickly child and perhaps because of this he was very spoiled. At school he was often naughty but his teachers were not allowed to cane him. Whenever Edward needed to be punished, another boy stepped forward to provide a substitute bottom. Despite this special treatment Edward didn't live to see his 16th birthday[11].

11 The cause of his death was said to be tuberculosis but the symptoms were very strange – he died bald and without fingernails.

Around this time, Europe was going through a religious revolution. In the 16th century, religion wasn't just a matter of personal choice, like supporting a football team, but a matter of life and death. Although almost everyone went to church and prayed to the same God, a growing number of people were very unhappy with the way the Pope and his supporters ran things. They thought they were too rich and out of touch with the people they were supposed to be serving. It sparked a huge argument between those who still thought that the Pope should be the leader of all Christians (Catholics) and those who thought the Pope had too much power (Protestants).

Edward was succeeded by his older sister Mary, who was Catholic. She wanted to return England to the way it was before her father Henry VIII split with Rome. But by this time a growing number of people at court and around the country had already become Protestants.

In Spain, where the king was also very Catholic, they had a ruthless way of dealing with Protestants. They tortured them in their thousands and if the victims didn't promise to become good Catholics, burned them at the stake. The Spanish Inquisition, as this terrible persecution of Protestants was called, was sweeping across Europe.

Mary, who was half-Spanish through her mother, loved everything Spanish and thought she would do her bit for the Inquisition. To show how committed she was to the Catholic cause, she even married the future king of Spain, Philip.

Mary's war against Protestantism brought horror and bloodshed to thousands, and many more fled into hiding. She would have gone on burning people alive if she hadn't died unexpectedly after just five years, when a lump in her stomach, which she thought was a baby, turned out to be a deadly tumour.

THE QUEEN WHO HAD A BATH ONCE A MONTH WHETHER SHE NEEDED ONE OR NOT

'Bloody' Mary was followed to the throne by her younger sister 'Good Queen Bess'. You could tell just by their nicknames that things were going to get better. And by and large things did get better – unless you were a Catholic.

After breaking from Catholicism under Henry VIII, then going Protestant under Edward VI, then going back to Catholicism under Queen Mary, England finally settled on Protestantism under the new Queen Elizabeth (1558-1603). No wonder people were confused.

Catholics were driven underground and were forced to practise their religion in secret rooms with priests smuggled in from abroad, wearing false beards. The penalty for hiding a Catholic priest was death.

When Elizabeth was young, she had long red hair and was thought beautiful, until she caught smallpox, leaving her badly scarred. For the rest of her life, she wore loads of heavy make-up to hide the pockmarks. Her favourite was a lead-based whitener that burned the skin, made your teeth rot and your hair fall out, and eventually resulted in death by lead poisoning. Elizabeth lost all her teeth and took to stuffing layers of cloth under her lips to fill out her face. She followed the fashion of the time, highlighting the veins on her chest in blue dye and wearing a hair gel made from a mixture of apples and puppy-dog fat. She once boasted that she had a bath once a month, 'whether I need it or not'. Towards the end of her reign, it was rumoured that she had grown a beard. And people wondered why she never got married.

Elizabeth was the first woman ever to try to run the country alone without a Prince Consort. Her advisers thought this was a mistake and that she would find it difficult to rule on her own.

To make her job even more difficult, there was also the tricky question of Elizabeth's claim to the throne. Her mother Anne Boleyn's marriage to her father Henry VIII was not approved by the Pope.

Elizabeth's Catholic cousin, Mary Queen of Scots, also had a good claim to the English throne. In 1571, the Pope Sixtus V took time off from burning Protestants to announce that he had just placed a huge bet on Mary becoming Queen of England – very soon, in fact. What's more, if a Catholic killed Elizabeth then God would definitely turn a blind eye. Given that at least half of Elizabeth's subjects *were* Catholic, it's not a surprise that quite a few decided to have a go. After all, if the Pope says it's okay, who's to argue?

Over the years, many plots to kill Elizabeth and replace her with Mary were uncovered. In 1586, Elizabeth's spies found a letter written to Mary by a group of seven young Catholics, offering to kill Elizabeth. Mary's written reply was also intercepted and decoded.

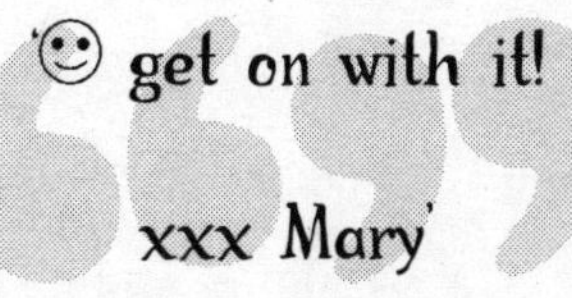

This time the government had a good excuse to get rid of Mary. Within days, the suspects were in chains being tortured into full confessions. For the Catholic plotters, death was as cruel as English law allowed. The first group of four was half-hanged and then their insides were ripped from their bodies while they were still alive. Elizabeth found reports of this so upsetting that it nearly put her off her breakfast, so she ordered that the next three were to be hanged until they were dead and only then cut down and quartered.

Mary was beheaded a week later, not in full view of thousands of witnesses on Tower Hill, but at Fotheringhay Castle in Northamptonshire, in front of just a few people.

It was a messy beheading. The executioner missed with his first stroke and hit the back of Mary's head, knocking her out. The second axe stroke sliced into the side of her skull, and the third finally chopped her head off. To the horror of everyone in the room, the headless body appeared to move; Mary's small pet dog had hidden itself under her long white dress. They had another big shock when the axeman picked up her severed head and her brown wig came away in his hand.

Elizabeth tried to pretend that her cousin's execution was a big mistake and just a game that got out of hand. But her former brother-in-law King Philip II of Spain, who knew a real execution when he saw one (he'd organised a few thousand himself) was not taken in by this story. He now had an excuse to launch his great Armada and sent 130 Spanish ships to invade England, get rid of Elizabeth and return the country to Catholicism.

At this point, the history books usually refer to a great naval victory won by Sir Francis Drake. In fact, on the English side, more sailors died from dysentery and typhoid than actual fighting. The Armada's chances of invading England were mostly wrecked by bad luck and terrible weather.

This convinced most English people that God was definitely on Elizabeth's side. The possibility of being hanged, drawn and quartered, or burnt alive, was enough to shut anyone up who might have questioned this line of argument.

Elizabeth reigned for 45 years and died aged 69, having survived lots of attempts to kill her, but not her make-up.

FOUL FACT

Elizabeth's mother, Anne Boleyn, had a habit, first noticed during her coronation banquet, of throwing up during meals. She employed a lady in waiting whose job it was to hold up a sheet when the Queen looked likely to puke.

THE KING WHO WAS AFRAID OF HIS OWN SHADOW

James I was the first person to be king of both England and Scotland. His family, the Stuarts, had ruled north of the border since 1371.

The Scottish Stuart kings had a habit of dying horribly. James I of Scotland was murdered while trying to escape through a stinking sewer, stabbed to death while up to his waist in sewage. James II died after standing too close to an exploding cannon, which sliced the top half of his head off. James III spent his entire reign worrying about a prophecy that he would be killed by an army led by his son; and so he was, in 1488. James IV died fighting the English at the battle of Flodden; afterwards his body was taken to England where his head was used as a football. James V caught a fever and died young just after another heavy defeat by the English. His only son was born in 1566.

> 'I know, let's call him James for good luck!'

King James VI of Scotland (and now James I of England) was a bow-legged little man with terrible personal habits. He slobbered when he ate and he never washed his hands, except for the very tips of his fingers, which he dabbed with a wet napkin. He was always fiddling with his codpiece and wore the same old vest until it was filthy and threadbare. He was very nervous and easily frightened. He was afraid of strangers, startled by loud noises, hated guns and was so terrified of violence he didn't even like to hear news of foreign wars. He was also terrified of witches and believed that a coven of witches was trying to kill him by whipping up a storm to sink his ship. The witches all confessed, after prolonged torture, and were burned at the stake.

There was of course a real plot to kill King James I, the most famous in British history – the Gunpowder Plot.

When he first came to the throne, a lot of Catholics thought the new king was going to give them a fair deal. However, it quickly became clear that under James, life for Catholics was going to be even worse. Very soon, a Catholic plot to kill the king was taking shape.

The king was due to open Parliament on 5th November, which gave the plotters enough time to collect a massive supply of gunpowder in a cellar directly underneath the room. One of the conspirators, Guy Fawkes, was given the job of lighting the fuse.

In the early hours of 4th November, Fawkes decided to visit the cellar one more time to check that the gunpowder was still in place, unaware that someone had tipped off the authorities and they were waiting to arrest him.

'That'll teach you never to return to an unexploded firework!'

Fawkes was arrested and searched and in his pockets they found a fuse and some matches. In the cellar were 36 barrels of gunpowder, enough to blow up the houses of Parliament 20 times over.

The others were tracked down to a house in Warwickshire where they tried to make a last stand in a dramatic shoot-out with the king's men. Unfortunately, they found that their gunpowder was damp, so someone had a bright idea.

'I know, let's put the gunpowder in front of the fire to dry it out'.

Which they did, accidentally blowing themselves up in the process.

They were the lucky ones. Guy Fawkes was tortured on the rack for three days before giving a full confession. His suffering can only be guessed at by the fact that he was several inches taller by the time they had finished with him.

King James set up a committee to see if they could come up with some form of death penalty that was even worse than hanging, drawing and quartering.

'How about hanging, drawing, quartering *and* tickling? That'll teach 'em!'

Despite their best efforts, three days later Guy Fawkes and three others were half-hanged, disembowelled and butchered in the usual way. Fawkes was the last to mount the scaffold, so weakened by torture he could barely stand.

The foiling of the Gunpowder Plot made King James very popular for a while, but it didn't last. He was even more fearful for his safety than before and for the rest of his reign he virtually gave up trying to rule. He spent his final days in bed, usually drunk, but always wearing his armoured vest.

THE KING WHO WAS 5’ 4” AT THE START OF HIS REIGN BUT ONLY 4’ 6” AT THE END OF IT

In 1612 it looked as though the future of the Stuart dynasty was in very good hands. King James’s eldest son, 18-year-old Henry, had everything you could hope for in a Prince of Wales. He was popular, handsome, witty, sporty and clever and a good Protestant. Then Henry suddenly dropped dead of typhoid fever. Unfortunately for everyone, his much less impressive younger brother Charles was now heir to the throne.

The day of Henry’s funeral was a time for great national mourning, which was slightly ruined by the fact that the king couldn’t be bothered to turn up (he hated funerals)

and then a streaker jumped out at the graveside, yelling that he was the dead prince's ghost.

Charles I was a poor replacement. Small, stunted by childhood rickets, bandy legged and painfully shy, he spoke with a stammer, which his parents tried to cure by making him talk with a mouthful of pebbles. He wasn't very bright either. This was obvious from his choice of bride, Queen Henrietta, who was described as having 'teeth coming out of her mouth like tusks.' She was also Roman Catholic *and* French, which made her very unpopular at the time. Just like his father, Charles thought he was appointed by God and therefore could do pretty much as he liked.

In the 1600s, Parliament's powers were very small compared to today. But Charles had very fixed ideas about his power. When Parliament refused to give Charles more money, the king simply closed Parliament down and ruled without it. Snubbed by a parliament he had never wanted anything to do with in the first place, the king decided to wage war on his own people.

In 1642, the country divided for Civil War – on one side were supporters of the king, known as the Royalists, and on the other were the Parliamentarians, known as the Roundheads.

What made the king's subjects choose sides? Many of those who fought for the Royalists didn't like the king very much, but felt bound to him by loyalty. Also, the Royalists had much better haircuts.

At first it looked as though the Royalists might win the Civil War, but then the Roundheads started to gain ground, led by their commander, Oliver Cromwell. In 1646 the king's army finally surrendered. The Roundheads had won.

Charles was seized and placed under guard, but Parliament didn't know what to do with him next. Cromwell wanted to put the king on trial, but there were others who thought that they should just send him on a holiday to somewhere hot. In June 1648, Cromwell finally got his own way and the king was tried for treason. Even now, not everyone realised that this would mean cutting his head off.

The idea of putting a king on trial was so new that nobody had a clue how to go about it. According to English law, a king could do no wrong, what with him being God's representative on earth and all that, and in theory nobody had the right to judge the king. Not even a judge. Still, they went ahead and put the king on trial anyway and just made it up as they went along.

Charles got over his stammer and spoke out clearly and defiantly; the 'court' had no authority to try him. Even at this late stage, many of the king's accusers probably did not intend to kill him and were hoping that the king would say 'sorry' and perhaps they could send him off on holiday after all, but the king's refusal to co-operate annoyed everyone.

Charles was found guilty as a 'tyrant, traitor, murderer, and a public enemy' and was sentenced to death. Royalty was officially cancelled.

In England and France, hanging was for the lower classes and only aristocrats were beheaded, the lucky beggars. To be honest though, being an aristocrat did not make death much more fun. Severing a head with a clean blow needed a lot of skill and even experienced axemen could take several blows to finish the job. Fortunately England's chief executioner Richard Brandon had had plenty of practice. He had always wanted to be a chief executioner, like his dad.

The king's execution on 30th January 1649 was scheduled for the morning and Charles thought he'd make a fashion statement by wearing two vests. Either that, or it was a bitterly cold day and he didn't want his subjects to see him shiver in case they thought he was shaking with fear. This was an age when Londoners saw lots of public executions and thought of them as a form of entertainment. But nobody had seen anything like this before.

Charles complained to the executioner when he saw how low the block was and realised that he would have to lie down to place his head on it. He cheered up a bit when the executioner helpfully pointed out that he wouldn't have to get up afterwards. Brandon brought his axe down on the king's neck and with one stroke, the British monarchy was ended.

FOUL FACT

During the Civil War, Cromwell's soldiers killed the Royalist general Sir Arthur Aston by beating him to death with his own wooden leg.

THE KING WHO PARTIED

For five years after the execution of Charles I Britain didn't have a king or queen. It was a republic ruled by Oliver Cromwell, but he was not a popular leader. He became even more unpopular when he banned Christmas. Shopkeepers were furious.

'Cutting the king's head off is one thing, but getting rid of Christmas? Honestly, he's gone too far now!'

When Cromwell died in 1658, the Royalists were in charge again. In 1660, on his 30th birthday, the former king's eldest son was warmly welcomed home as Charles II. All of the official documents were backdated so that the new king's reign started on the day the old one finished – as though Oliver Cromwell and the republic had never happened.

England was overjoyed to have a king once more but Parliament saw to it that there was no return to the old days, when the king or queen could order everyone around as he saw fit. Charles didn't mind, he was too busy having a good time going to the theatre, the races, or chasing butterflies.

But there was also some unfinished business with the people who signed his father's death warrant. Most of them had their heads chopped off in a single week in 1660. The body of Oliver Cromwell was dug up, hanged, then dumped in a pit. His head was dipped in tar then set on a spike on top of Westminster Hall, where it stayed until it was blown down by a gale in 1703.[12]

At first, Charles II was a very popular king, but his reign was not without problems. In 1665, the Great Plague killed about 100,000 people, including 70,000 in London. Charles didn't hang around to see the suffering – he and his court fled to Oxford, where they had a great time partying. Meanwhile, Londoners were forced to stay indoors until they died.

12 Cromwell's skull has changed hands several times. At one time there were two 'genuine' Cromwell skulls on sale in London at the same time. The owner of the second, smaller skull explained that his version was that of Cromwell when he was a boy!

In 1666, even more disaster followed when the Great Fire destroyed most of London. Some people thought this was God's way of punishing the country for the king's sinful ways and wondered if things were really so bad under Cromwell after all.

All things considered, Charles II wasn't a great king, but unlike his father, who was rude, he was charming and very likeable. This meant that people forgave him for almost anything, even when it was rumoured that he might secretly be a Catholic. Which he was, but he had the good sense to keep quiet about it right up until his death.

FOUL FACT

London's messiest execution took place on 15th July 1685 when the king's son, the Duke of Monmouth, went under the axe at Tower Hill for treason. The Duke was heard to complain loudly that the axeman's blade looked a bit blunt, but nobody took any notice. Eventually, the fifth blow finally severed the Duke's head from his shoulders, just before he had a chance to say 'I told you so'.

THE KING WHO WAS KILLED BY A MOLE

When Parliament cut off the head of King Charles I, they were also sending out a message that they got to decide who became king or queen from now on. So when James II came to the throne and tried to make the country Catholic again, Parliament simply got rid of him and offered the crown to his Protestant daughter Mary – and her Dutch husband William of Orange.

Mary was the first British queen to rule jointly with her husband, so the reign is always known as that of William III and Mary II, but he did most of the ruling. Although to be fair, there wasn't all that much ruling to be done. The king and queen were now controlled by Parliament and weren't allowed to make any important decisions, like changing the law or going to war. These rules are still present in Britain today.

'So, if we're not actually ruling, what are we supposed to do with our time?'

'Well, you could take up hunting?'

'Hmm. Not sure about that, I heard it didn't go too well for William II'.

'Good point. What about visiting schools, going to royal variety shows, that sort of thing? You could even do a speech on Christmas Day'.

'All right, we'll give it a whirl.'

In centuries past, royal weddings must have been quite a thrill – unless you were actually taking part in them. William and Mary's was probably one of the least romantic royal weddings ever. He was 27, and she was just 15. He was also said to be very ugly – small, weedy and very hunched, with a hooked nose and terrible asthma. Mary burst into tears when she saw him for the first time and spent the whole of the wedding ceremony crying.

Mary died young from smallpox in 1694 and was widely mourned. William ruled alone after that but he was never really liked. His English was poor, he had awful table manners and he seemed to be more interested in Holland than in England. They liked him a bit more when he defeated England's old arch-rival France, but not a lot. He died in 1702, after being thrown from his horse when it stumbled on a molehill.

THE QUEEN WHO WAS AS WIDE AS SHE WAS TALL

William and Mary didn't have any children, so the crown passed to Mary's younger sister Anne. In 1707, the Acts of Union combined England and Scotland into a single kingdom, so Anne also became the first ruling monarch of Great Britain.

Anne was one of the unhealthiest monarchs ever. She suffered from arthritis and gout, which made her joints painful and swollen, and although she was tiny – only 4' 9" tall – by the time of her coronation she weighed about 20st and had to be carried into Westminster Abbey in a chair. She hated any form of exercise and was happy to be dragged around her palace on chairs with wheels and pulleys.

Drinking tea became very popular during her reign and ever since then, all Englishmen are said to fancy a 'nice hot cup of tea'. However, Queen Anne preferred something a lot stronger – hence her nickname Brandy

Nan. She spent all her time playing cards with her ladies-in-waiting, drinking and eating. The French ambassador was astonished by the amount of food she could eat and was afraid that 'she might burst'. She had a lot in common with her husband Prince George, who was also a big drinker and was said to be very dull. It was joked that George was so boring that his asthma attacks were the only way you could tell that he was still alive.

Anne had 13 children. Sadly, they all died before she did. Only one, William, made it through infancy. He died at the age of 11, it was said, from too much dancing on his birthday.

By the time of Anne's death at age 49, she was so fat that her coffin was almost square. Her death left one very strange and permanent mark on the country. Until 1714, when a judge wore his robes in court he had several different colour options. When Anne died, the colour was changed to black, because the judges were in official mourning for the queen, and they have stayed that way ever since.

THE KING WHO SPOKE ONLY GERMAN

The fact that Queen Anne had no surviving children was a terrible tragedy for her, but it was also bad news for the country. There was a law banning Catholics from sitting on the throne, so that ruled out another 56 of Anne's nearest Stuart relatives. After a long search, they found her closest Protestant relative was a middle-aged German duke from Hanover, who was as surprised as anyone when he suddenly became King George I of Great Britain and Ireland.

At 54, George figured that he was too old to pick up any British culture, so he spent most of his time avoiding it by going back to Hanover whenever he could. He didn't speak English and couldn't be bothered to learn any and his ministers didn't speak any German either, so they had to communicate with each other in Latin. As George was away so often, his ministers found that they could run the country quite well without him – so the job of Prime Minister was created for someone who could act on the king's behalf.

After ruling England for 13 years, George I died of a stroke on one of his frequent trips back to Hanover.

FOUL FACT

Dwarfs, for anyone who could afford to keep them, were the 18th century television; if you were royalty you had one in every room. George I had a court dwarf called Christian Ulrich Jorry, a gift from a German nobleman, who entertained the king and his friends at supper parties.

THE QUEEN WHOSE BOWELS EXPLODED

Just like his father, George II was badly educated and bad mannered. He also suffered terribly from piles, again just like his father, and had to have a very painful operation to have them removed.[13]

13 The British National Anthem 'God Save The King (or Queen) has been around since the reign of George II, but the song itself is much older. According to one story it was written in 1686 by some French nuns to celebrate King Louis XIV's recovery from an operation on his piles. Co-incidence or what?

George was very vain and very touchy about his problem and tried to keep it a secret from everyone, including his servants. When one of his Lords of the Bedchamber asked him how he was feeling, George sacked him on the spot.

However, he was very brave and was the very last British king to lead his troops into battle – at Dettingen against the French in 1743 – even though he was nearly 60 years old. During the battle, he nearly had his head blown off by a cannon ball.

George also had enough sense to listen to his clever wife, Queen Caroline. When the king's ministers needed the king to do something, they went to his wife because she was the one with the brains and the king usually did whatever she told him to do. Caroline was a very modern queen. Unlike Queen Anne, who still believed she could cure illness through some kind of magic called 'the royal touch', Caroline put her faith in science. She even had her own children protected against smallpox by the new method of vaccination. This was generally thought to be a very courageous thing and set a fine example, although what her children thought about being used as guinea pigs is another matter.

'Sorry Mum, just for a moment there
I thought you said we're going to be
injected with the pus from the weeping
sore of a scabby smallpox victim.'

'I did. Now eat your greens'.

In the end it was Caroline who suffered most horribly from 18th century medical science. In 1737, she was overcome by a terrible stomach pain and her doctors decided to operate on her. Caroline endured the surgery bravely, without any anaesthetic, and she even laughed out loud when the surgeon stood too close to a candle and set fire to his wig. A little while after her operation, as she lay in bed surrounded by courtiers, her bowels exploded, showering poo all over the bed and the floor. After a long silence one of her courtiers said that she hoped the almighty poo would do her majesty some good.

The Queen replied that she hoped so too, because it was the last she would ever have. She died soon afterwards and when the poet Alexander Pope heard the gruesome details he wrote:

> 'Here lies wrapt in forty
> thousand towels
> The only proof that Caroline
> had bowels.'

George outlived his wife by 23 years. Death came to him on the toilet, when he was 67. His German servant heard a noise which was a lot louder than the king's usual fart and found him slumped dead on the floor. He had had a heart attack while straining to overcome his constipation!

FOUL FACT

When Queen Victoria inherited Buckingham Palace in 1837 it didn't even have a bathroom. The Georgian royals believed it was 'sweat that kept a man clean'.

THE KING WHO TALKED TO A TREE

Two Georges down and two to go. The latest monarchy didn't have much imagination when it came to naming their children. In fact there should have been a King Fred, but George II's eldest son never made it to the throne – he died after being hit on the head by a cricket ball.

So when George II fell off his toilet seat in 1760, the crown passed to his 22-year-old grandson, George III, whose reign would become the longest of all the British kings. He was also the first George who could speak English properly, so the people he ruled could understand him – or at least they could while he was still sane.

George III's long reign is chiefly remembered in two ways. The first is that he was 'the king who lost the American colonies' – which, let's be honest, was careless of him. We're talking about an area of 360,000 square miles of land where most of the population of North America lived – not the sort of thing you lose down the back of the sofa. To be fair, George had very little say in this, because the colonies declared their independence in the American Revolution and went off to form the United States, so he's not really to blame.

The second thing George is remembered for is that he was the king who went 'mad'. In the late 1780s, he took to wearing a pillowcase on his head and began foaming at the mouth. The story goes that one day he got out of the royal coach and went to talk to an oak tree, thinking it was the King of Prussia. At first his courtiers tried to keep his illness a secret from the outside world by pretending that the king had flu, but the cat was out of the bag when the king began his address to the House of Commons, 'My Lords and Peacocks'. It was a tricky time for everyone, especially the poor Poet Laureate, who was expected to write a cheerful poem every year about the king on his birthday.

Eventually George was too mad even to be trusted to perform even the basic royal tasks like waving from the balcony at Buckingham Palace. In October 1810, shortly after celebrations to mark the 72-year-old king's Golden Jubilee, he was laced into a straitjacket and packed off to Windsor Castle, where he spent the last few years of his life blind and deaf.

FOUL FACT

The Georgians had several theories as to what might have sent the king mad. Some thought it was losing the American colonies. His doctors thought he was suffering from 'flying gout', a strange illness that started in the feet and was thought to be quite harmless unless you were unlucky enough to get it in your head. The strangest theory of all was that his condition was brought on by having a very ugly wife.

THE KING WHO ATE ALL THE (PIGEON) PIES

One of the most liked British monarchs was followed by one of the most hated – George IV.

The fourth George's reign, including the time known as the Regency period when he reigned while his father was mad, is remembered as a great time for British art, fashion and culture. And it was a great time if you could afford to enjoy it. For most people it was a time of real hardship. Britain was at war with France (again), people were losing their jobs, there was rioting in the streets and ordinary Britons were struggling to feed their families.

But not King George IV – he was spending huge sums of money and running up enormous debts. His selfish ways first became obvious to everyone when he celebrated becoming king, with the most expensive Coronation Banquet anyone had ever seen, a marathon of eating that caused so much offence that it was the very last event of its kind.

By this time George was already middle-aged and very fat and was known as the 'Prince of Whales' thanks to his 54 inch waist. For breakfast he had two pigeons and three beef steaks, washed down with brandy and champagne.[14] He was too fat to climb up the palace stairs and had to sleep on the ground floor. And while George was chomping on his pigeon McNuggets and sloshing them down with a bucketful of champagne, many of his subjects were actually starving.

Although very fat, George was also very vain and tried to make himself look slimmer by cramming his stomach into corsets drawn in by a huge belt. He was also very touchy about his weight. Although he owned the biggest backside ever to sit on the British throne (despite some stiff competition from Queen Anne) he had the poet Leigh Hunt thrown into prison for daring to call him 'fat'.

Some people thought that he was a bit mad – like his father. He told very tall stories, like the one about his bravery at the Battle of Waterloo; according to George,

---

14 Yes, the Georgians did have some surprising ideas about healthy eating, but at least it was good to see that the king was getting his five wildfowl a day.

he actually led a cavalry charge. This was obviously a massive lie because he had never once been anywhere near the fighting.

Another reason for George IV's unpopularity was his long-running row with his wife Queen Caroline. Arranged royal marriages were often unhappy affairs but this was worst than most. They didn't get to meet until three days before the wedding. When he first clapped eyes on her he said 'I feel ill, get me a brandy' – which has to be one of the worst chat up lines in history.

To be fair, Caroline was very scruffy, smelly, unwashed and she swore a lot. She wasn't too impressed with him either; she described him as 'very fat and nothing like as handsome as his portrait'. On his wedding day he went through the ceremony 'looking like death' and at one point tried to run off, but was held back by his father. After that George and Caroline went their own separate ways.

For the rest of his reign, George was jeered at and his coach pelted with mud by London mobs every time he dared to go outside. In the end he stopped going out and shut himself away in his bedroom, spending the last eight years of his reign hiding away at Windsor Castle.

When George IV died, there were no tears at his funeral, but there was quite a lot of gasping and choking. Something had gone wrong with the embalming process, so his already bloated body became even more swollen and almost burst through the lead lining in his coffin. Luckily, someone stepped forward and drilled a hole in it to let out some of the bad air before it was too late. George IV's funeral had been a bit like his reign – a pretty horrible experience.

THE KING WITH THE PINEAPPLE-SHAPED HEAD

George IV died without having any children, so in 1830 the crown passed to his brother William IV, who became king at the age of 64 – the oldest person ever to become a British monarch.

William liked to be known as the Sailor King because he once served in the navy, but most of the time people called him 'pineapple head'.

'I'm the Sailor King. What's all this nonsense about fruit?

'Well your Majesty, your head does look just a tiny bit, you know, pineapple-shaped.'

On the inside of his head, there didn't seem to be a lot going on. Even by Hanoverian standards, he was a bit of a fool. On the rare occasions when he had to do anything important, like speak to the House of Commons, his

speeches were so rambling and confused that people thought he might be a bit mad as well. There was more evidence of oddness, like his habit of spitting in public, and when he invited people to dinner at the palace, he told his guests not to 'bother about clothes.' But hey! This was still so much better than having George IV as king.

William's weird head shape and even weirder behaviour may explain why he had some trouble finding himself a wife. After proposing to and being turned down by eight different women, he found a bride at last in Princess

Adelaide, who was described as 'frightful... very ugly with a horrid complexion'.

William died after just under seven years on the throne. The *Spectator* wrote: 'His late Majesty, though at times a jovial and, for a king, an honest man, was a weak, ignorant, commonplace sort of person.' Ouch!

In the end, the single most important thing about William's reign was that he and Queen Adelaide didn't have any surviving children. So now the crown would pass to his 18-year-old niece – Queen Victoria.

THE QUEEN WHO HID FROM HER SUBJECTS

By the time 18-year-old Victoria came to the throne all anyone could remember was being ruled over by middle-aged men, so the young queen was a nice change.

Victoria was very small and dumpy and by the end of her reign she had grown quite round. She was always worried about her health and would call for her doctor up to half a dozen times a day with various imaginary complaints, usually about her stomach. On his honeymoon, he was surprised to receive a message from the queen, which informed him 'the bowels are acting fully'.

Three years after she became queen, she married her German cousin Prince Albert of Saxe-Coburg-Gotha. She adored him and they had nine children. Her subjects were less keen on Albert.

Victoria was lucky to be queen during one of the most successful periods of British history. She no longer ruled over a small island off the edge of Europe, as William the Conqueror had done, but the biggest empire the world had ever seen.

But not everyone felt good about their queen. She survived six attempts to kill her – a record she shares with the Russian Czar Alexander II (who was finally blown to pieces on the seventh attempt in 1881).

Britain was the world's biggest superpower, but the gap between the rich and the poor was massive and life was grim for most of Victoria's subjects. It wasn't a healthy place to live either. Although the queen herself lived to a ripe old age, most Britons were lucky if they reached their late forties.

When Albert died in 1861, she was so upset that she shut herself away for more than 25 years, wearing only black mourning clothes. Every day until she died Albert's clothes were laid out at Windsor and a bowl of hot water was prepared for him to shave – more than a little bit spooky! A whole generation grew up grumbling that they had never seen the queen. There was even scandalous gossip that she had secretly married her Scottish manservant John Brown.

The queen was eventually persuaded to come out of hiding for her Golden Jubilee in 1887, to celebrate her 50th year on the throne. After that, she started to appear in public again and she became a national icon. When Victoria died of old age in 1901, after the longest reign in British history[15], the Victorian era died with her.

FOUL FACT

Meal times with Victoria were very hard on her guests. The queen was always served first, and she always started eating as soon as the food arrived. As soon as she had finished, her servants took away everyone's plates. At big banquets, many of her guests could go hungry!

15 The world record is held by Louis XIV of France, who was crowned when he was four and reigned for 72 years.

FOUL FACT

Jack Black was Victoria's longest serving Royal Rat and Mole Destroyer. Although he was nearly killed three times by rats and once found that a rat had bitten clean through a bone in his finger, Black didn't mind because he got to eat as many rats as he could take home with him. Rats, he said, were 'moist as rabbits and twice as nice'.

THE KING WHO SHOT THINGS

When Victoria died in 1901, her last word was 'Bertie'. This was the name of her eldest son, named after her beloved husband Albert. It was her dying wish that Bertie was crowned King Albert I – so he called himself King Edward VII just to annoy her.

Edward didn't get on with his parents, who thought he was a huge disappointment. Unlike his sensible, hard working father, Edward was very fond of wine and cigars. It also didn't help that Albert died of typhoid just after they had a huge row. It is said the queen thought her son was partly responsible for Albert's death and she never forgot this.

Edward was 60 by the time he became king. His first job was to go around smashing all the photos and statues of John Brown that his mother had placed around the palace. His second was to install some proper flushing toilets.

Edward was immensely fat. When he wasn't eating, he liked to shoot things. He was a rubbish shot, so tame birds were driven over him just a few feet above his head, to ensure he couldn't miss. When he became too old and fat to walk, he had deer driven directly at him, straight down the barrel of his gun. He once sent an excited message to his mother from Nepal: 'Shot an elephant and wounded severely two others'. He also had another rather weird hobby – he recorded the weight of everyone who ever visited his home.

A lifetime of too much eating and drinking finally caught up with him when he died of heart failure aged 68 at Buckingham Palace on 6th May 1910, having reigned for only nine years.

FOUL FACT

Edward VII enjoyed shooting wild animals but he was a useless shot. One day he accidentally shot his own brother-in-law Prince Christian in the face. Christian had to have an eye removed. This encouraged him to start a collection of glass eyes, which he liked to bring out and show people at dinner parties. His favourite was a bloodshot one which he wore when he had a cold.

THE QUEEN WHO STOLE THINGS

George V became king because his older brother Albert Victor had died of pneumonia. Not only did he get his brother's crown, he also got his fiancée, Mary.

By the time of George's reign, Britain's position as the world superpower was being challenged by Germany. It seemed certain that there would be a war to see who was top dog. The fact that the king and Germany's leader Kaiser Wilhelm were first cousins didn't make any difference. When the two countries went to war in 1914, there was a lot of anti-German feeling. German shopkeepers in London had their windows smashed and their goods stolen, and people refused to drink German wine. It was time someone had a quiet word with the king.

So it was decided that the Royal House of Saxe-Coburg-Gotha would be renamed to sound more English. The king suggested the House of Wipper, then the House of

Wettin. When everyone had stopped laughing, he settled for Windsor.

George V began the tradition of making a Christmas Day broadcast to the nation (on the exciting new invention called a radio). It made him very popular with his people. It was around this time that people first started talking fondly about the Royal Family.[16] George liked to present himself as someone ordinary people could identify with – which to be fair you could, as long as you'd won the Lottery and had decided to spend all your time shooting wild animals.

The king's other hobby was stamp-collecting. His wife Queen Mary was said to have had a more worrying hobby; she stole things. It usually happened in other people's homes. While out visiting, apparently she would slip any small item she took a fancy to – like a small ornament – into her handbag. Everyone would pretend it hadn't happened and her ladies-in-waiting would usually return the items later when the Queen wasn't looking.

George V was the last British monarch to be murdered, although few people knew it at the time. When he lay

16 Not something that you would have heard said about Edward VII's family, especially since one of his sons was suspected of being Jack the Ripper!

dying in 1936, the royal doctor finished him off with a large lethal injection, just so that news of the king's death would be in time to make the headlines in *The Times* the next morning!

FOUL FACT

George V once shot and killed 39 tigers in a single day. This didn't stop him claiming that he was an animal lover! To prove it, he had a pet parrot who was allowed to roam around the palace, dropping pellets everywhere, including the breakfast table. George would slide a mustard pot over the poo and carry on eating.

THE KING WHO BARELY WAS

When Edward VIII became king, he was already very popular. During the First World War he had served in the army and he went on loads of trips around the world on his father's behalf. The monarchy under his father had become a bit stuffy and formal, but Edward was going to shake things up and do it his way. Like facing the wrong way on his coins. Whatever next?

People thought he was going to be a good king. This was based mostly on a visit he made to some poor people in South Wales. When he saw their living conditions, he was shocked to find they were not up to Palace standards, and muttered 'something must be done'. Nothing ever was, not by Edward anyway, but it's the thought that counts.

By now he was the most photographed celebrity of the time. For the first 10 months of his reign, the new king was incredibly popular, then one day…

'Hang on, who is that woman with the king?'

Her name was Mrs. Wallace Simpson and she was an American divorcée and a commoner – i.e. not royal. And the king wanted to marry her.

Now there is no rule that says the king has to marry someone royal, or one that says he can't marry a divorcée. In fact Henry VIII had pretty much fixed it so that a king could marry anyone he wanted to – which he did six times, including four commoners.[17]

But everyone was so scandalised that there was a Facebook campaign to have the then king removed from the throne – or there would have been if social networking had been invented. The Prime Minister told Edward that if he wanted to marry Mrs. Simpson, he would have to give up the throne. Edward got the message and resigned before he was even crowned.[18] His younger brother Bertie was

17 But there is, strangely enough, still a law that says the king can't marry a Catholic – the 1701 Act of Settlement.

18 But he still counts as a British monarch because he became king at the very minute his father died.

crowned King George VI in his place. Edward married Mrs. Simpson and they went on an extended holiday that lasted for the rest of their lives.

These days nobody would complain if the king married a divorcée – in fact our future king Prince Charles already has.

THE KING WHO CURED HIS STAMMER (BUT NOT HIS SMOKING HABIT)

Like Charles I, King George VI was very shy and had a terrible stammer. But whereas Charles's stammer was completely cured by cutting off his head, George went to see a speech therapist.

In 1939, Britain was at war with Germany once again. This time there was no confusion about the king's surname and whose side they might be on, so Adolf Hitler made a point of bombing Buckingham Palace nine times.

When German bombs started to rain down on London every night, the king and queen went down to the East End to see the terrible damage for themselves. They also insisted on staying in London so that ordinary people could see that the royal family were doing their bit.[19]

When Britain eventually won the war, a million people crowded on to the Mall to cheer the royal family, who stood on the palace balcony and waved. The Prime Minister Winston Churchill said that future generations would look back at the early part of World War II, when Britain had stood completely alone against the evil of Nazism, and say 'this was their finest hour'.

This was also one of the finest hours of Britain's royal family because they, including their young daughter the future Queen Elizabeth, had never been more popular. Unfortunately George was a heavy smoker and he smoked himself to death aged just 56.

FOUL FACT

King George's grandfather Edward VII had a golf bag made from an elephant's willy. It was a present from an Indian maharajah.

19 Or that's what everyone was told. In fact the king and queen secretly slipped away from London and slept every night at Windsor.

THE QUEEN WHO WENT UP A TREE A PRINCESS AND CAME DOWN A QUEEN

Elizabeth II[20] became queen while sitting in a tree in Africa, watching a rhinoceros drinking from a pool.

People liked her straight away, especially when they got used to singing God Save the *Queen* instead of *King*. Her coronation ceremony was the first to be watched on TV by millions of people all around the world.

At the time she was already married to Prince Philip, whose surname Schleswig-Holstein-Sonderburg-Glücksburg, was a bit of a mouthful, so he was persuaded to change it to the Duke of Edinburgh to save time.

---

20 In Scotland she is Elizabeth I, because England's first Elizabeth wasn't Queen in Scotland.

The kingdom that Elizabeth inherited was very different from the one she rules today. We don't own a worldwide Empire any more. But many of Britain's old colonies wanted to keep her as their queen, which meant she had to travel all over the world eating strange things (at a state dinner during her visit to Belize in 1985 she was even fed roasted rat) and waving to people. And everywhere the Queen goes, it is said that her personal lavatory seat cover made of white leather goes too.

Today Elizabeth II is one of the biggest (if not *the* biggest) celebrity in the world. The Queen can trace her ancestors back to the Saxe-Coburg-Gothas, and before them the Hanovers, then the Stuarts, Tudors, Yorkists,

Lancastrians, Plantagenets, Normans and so on, all the way back to Alfred the Great. And there's more than a bit of Viking in there too.

The monarchy has changed a lot over the past 2000 years. For a start, you don't risk having your ears and tongues ripped out and your hands chopped off for being slightly disrespectful to the Queen any more. And William the Conqueror didn't keep corgis.

Britain has had every kind of king and queen you can imagine – stupid, clever, greedy, generous, brave, cowardly, good, mad, bad and deadly dangerous. Thanks to Elizabeth II, you can add at least two more qualities to this list – dutiful and dignified. And 'very important for tourism'.

In May 2011, Elizabeth II became the second longest reigning monarch in British history (after Victoria who held the throne for more than 63 years) and there's still no sign of her slowing up yet. On 10 September 2015, she should become the longest-serving British monarch ever and still as popular as the day she began her job.

FOUL FACT

Apparently, the Queen's favourite royal story, according to those in the know, was about the time she shared a horse-drawn carriage with a visiting African president. During the trip one of the Queen's horses farted so loudly that it couldn't be ignored, so the Queen apologised to her guest. He whispered back 'that's quite all right Ma'am... I thought it was the horse.'

TIMELINE

William I 'the Conqueror' (1066 – 1087)

p3

William II (1087 – 1100)

p7

Henry I (1100 – 1135)

p10

Edward III (1327 – 1377)

p29

Richard II (1377 – 1399)

p33

Henry IV (1399 – 1413)

p37

Henry V (1413 – 1422)

p39

Henry VI (1422-61, 1470-71)

Edward IV (1461-70, 1471-1483)

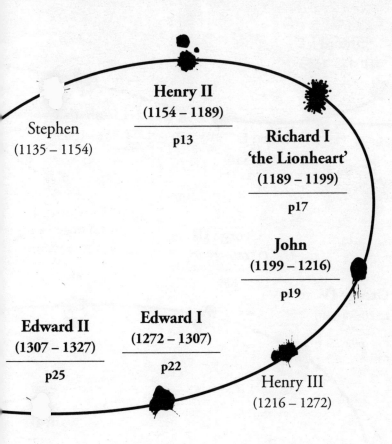

Stephen
(1135 – 1154)

Henry II
(1154 – 1189)
p13

Richard I
'the Lionheart'
(1189 – 1199)
p17

John
(1199 – 1216)
p19

Henry III
(1216 – 1272)

Edward I
(1272 – 1307)
p22

Edward II
(1307 – 1327)
p25

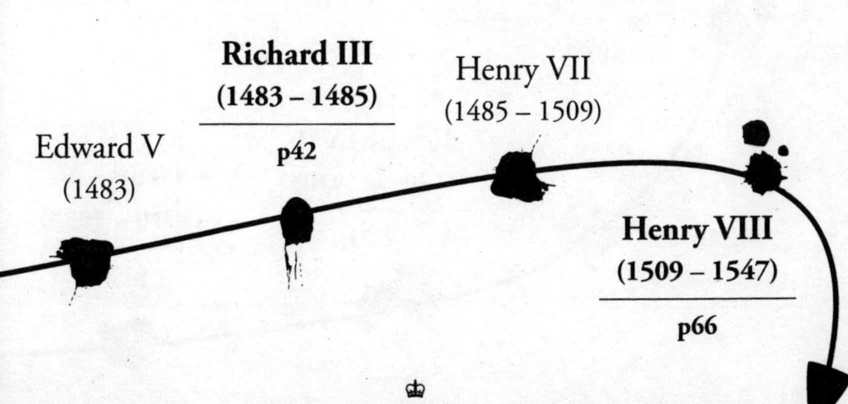

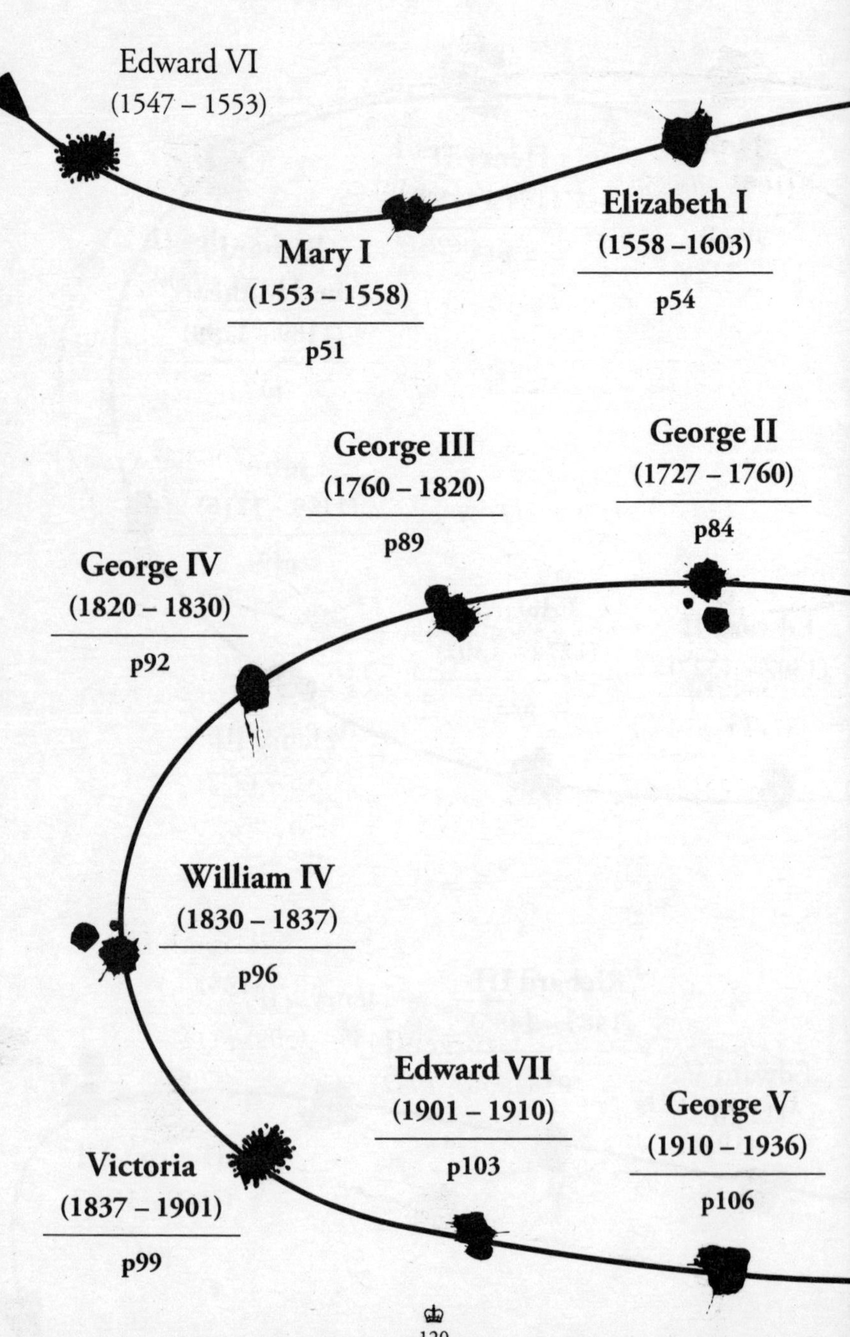
Edward VI
(1547 – 1553)
Mary I
(1553 – 1558)
p51
Elizabeth I
(1558 –1603)
p54
George III
(1760 – 1820)
p89
George II
(1727 – 1760)
p84
George IV
(1820 – 1830)
p92
William IV
(1830 – 1837)
p96
Edward VII
(1901 – 1910)
p103
George V
(1910 – 1936)
p106
Victoria
(1837 – 1901)
p99

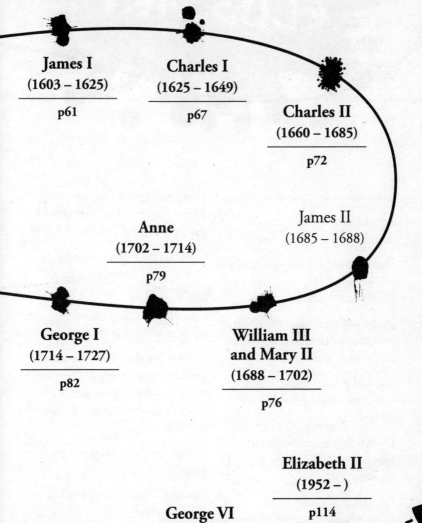

James I
(1603 – 1625)
p61

Charles I
(1625 – 1649)
p67

Charles II
(1660 – 1685)
p72

James II
(1685 – 1688)

William III
and Mary II
(1688 – 1702)
p76

Anne
(1702 – 1714)
p79

George I
(1714 – 1727)
p82

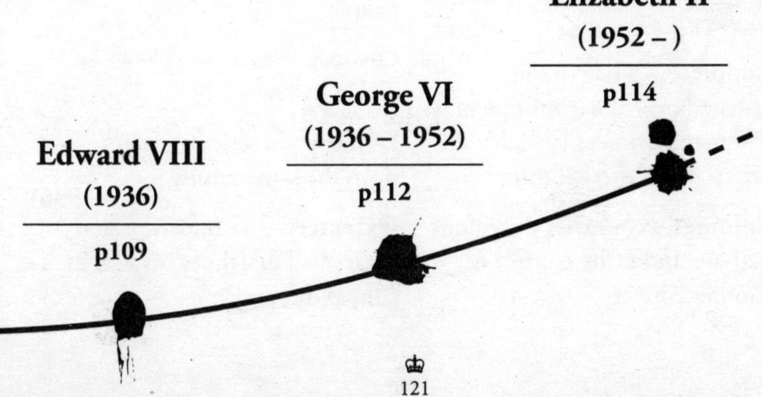

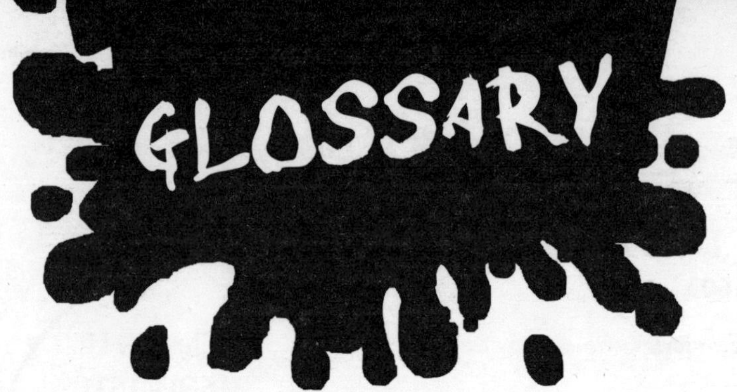

Accuracy – being true or exact

Aristocrats – noblemen or members of the royal family

Bankrupted – completely run out of money and declared by law to have none

Bribe – money or a gift given to someone to encourage them to do what you want

Capital punishment – killing someone to punish them for a crime

Civil war – a war between groups of people in the same country

Codpiece – a bag or flap fastened over the front opening of a man's trousers (which were very tight in the 1500s!)

Colonies – countries or regions that are under the control of another country

Conquering – a king or queen taking control of a country by the use of force

Coronation – the crowning ceremony of a new king or queen

Courtiers – companions or advisers to the king or queen

Crown Jewels – valuable items used in coronations throughout history, including crowns, rings and swords covered with precious stones

Debts – money owed to other people

Divorce – when a marriage is ended by law

Dynasty – a series of rulers from the same family

Dysentery – an infection that causes bad diarrhoea, as well as pain and fever

Excommunicated – banned from being a member of the church and from attending any of the religious ceremonies there

Feuding – violent quarrelling

Gangrene – an infection leading to death of body tissue, often in one particular limb

Jester – a professional clown or 'joker' at a royal court

Jury – a group of people who will look at the evidence for a crime during a trial and give a verdict of 'innocent' or 'guilty'

Longbows – large bows, sometimes more than 1.8 metres (6 feet) long, that shot feathered arrows

Looting – stealing during a riot or war

Maharajah – an Indian king or prince

Monastery – a place where a group of monks live and work

Mutilated – having a limb cut off

Nazism – a movement started by Adolf Hitler in Germany. The Nazis thought they were superior to other races

Parliament – a national body that has powers to make laws

Persecution – causing harm to someone because of their beliefs

Pudding-bowl – an unfashionable haircut looking as if a bowl has been put on someone's head and the hair cut round it

Rickets – a disease caused by lack of vitamin D or calcium, causing problems with bone formation

Smallpox – an often fatal disease, causing fever and blisters all over the skin

Subjects – people under the rule of a king or queen

Treason – the act of plotting to harm or overthrow the king or queen

Typhoid fever – an infection often due to salmonella bacteria, which causes diarrhoea and a rash

Vaccination – injecting someone with a weak version of an illness-causing virus or bacteria. This protects them from the illness

INDEX